1⁰⁰

D0331574

MEDIT/
WITH ™
MECHTILD
of
MAGDEBURG

Versions by
SUE WOODRUFF

Preface by
MATTHEW FOX

Bear & Company
Santa Fe, New Mexico

Copyright © 1982 by Bear & Company, Inc.

ISBN 0-939680-06-8

Library of Congress Card Number 82-73366

All rights reserved. No part of this book may be reproduced by any means and in any form whatsoever without written permission from the publisher.

Bear & Company, Inc.
P.O. Drawer 2860
Santa Fe, NM 87504

Typography: Casa Sin Nombre, Santa Fe

Cover art & line illustrations: Sue Woodruff

Printed in the United States by George Banta Company, Inc.

Contents

Publisher's Note

Bear & Company is publishing this series of creation-centered mystic/prophets to bring to the attention and prayer of peoples today the power and energy of the holistic mystics of the western tradition. One reason western culture succumbs to boredom and to violence is that we are not being challenged by our religious traditions to be all we can be. This is also the reason that many sincere spiritual seekers go East for their mysticism—because the West is itself out of touch with its deepest spiritual guides. The format Bear & Company has chosen in which to present these holistic mystic/prophets is deliberate: We do not feel that more academically-styled books on our mystics is what every-day believers need. Rather, we wish to get the mystics of personal and social transformation off our dusty shelves and into the hearts and minds and bodies of our people. To do this we choose a format that is ideal for meditation, for imaging, for sharing in groups and in prayer occasions. We rely on primary sources for the texts but we let the author's words and images flow from her or his inner structure to our deep inner selves.

Preface

It is a great privilege to welcome Mechtild of Magdeburg (1210-c.1280) into our hearts and lives once again. For this I am very grateful to Sue Woodruff for her hard work and deep commitment to Mechtild and her vision. It is a vision that has been sorely lacking in male-dominated culture and religion in the West for hundreds of years. In this brief preface I would like to praise Mechtild for her spiritual vision that can nurture and challenge us who suffer from so much brokenness, violence and dualism in the latter part of the twentieth century.

1. Let us praise Mechtild for her willingness to live an alternative lifestyle. Mechtild spent most of her long, active, adult life as a Beguine. Beguines were for the most part women of the lower classes who lived together and worked for a living but did not become nuns and did not marry. They were often a threat to those in power, having been condemned and then not-condemned by the Pope, being welcomed and then driven out by bishops. Sociologically, the movement is due in part to the fact that the crusades created a situation in Germany where a shortage of men existed. Women learned to get along without them and became Beguines. They were nurtured by solid Scriptural studies and compassionate service of the oppressed. In many respects they lived lives of "base communities" as many Christians are learning to do today. For today too a panoply of crusades have rendered a shortage of good men in many places: Crusades of imperialism, anti-communism, machoism—all these crusades have often rendered women without authentic relationships with men. Like the Beguines and Mechtild, such women are driven to live out the mystery of letting go and letting be in their lifestyles. In this difficult vocation Mechtild both helps and encourages. But she resists all effort to comfort by way of sentimentalizing. She exhorts, urging women and men alike on to fuller and deeper living. She does not countenance self-pity.

5

2. Let us praise Mechtild for her writing from deep feeling that avoids sentimentalism. Indeed, she offers us a way to delineate between passion and authentic feeling on the one hand and sentimentalism on the other. What is the line of demarcation between the two? True feeling, Mechtild demonstrates, leads to action. Yes, and to admitting anger but in making anger work for us. Sentimentalism, on the other hand, represses anger and turns it inwards. It reduces life to trivia. It wallows in emotion to the detriment of action. Mechtild urges people to fight against pain and suffering and not to succumb to it, much less to build a religion on it. True feeling, Mechtild insists, leads to creativity. Yes, she says, "we will have a creative kingdom!" She insists that people can and must change, let go, be transformed at profound levels. She entertains both positive and negative feelings and insists that God is present in both. She does not moralize about feelings but listens to them and acts out of them. In this respect Mechtild shows deep strains of being what we have called in the twentieth century an "existentialist." She begins with what is and trusts her experience, urging us to do the same when she says: "No one knows what comfort or desire or suffering is if she has not experienced them."

Mechtild does not only urge that we "loose those who are bound" and "care for the broken" but she says: "Thou shalt exhort the free." This is evidence that she is not pain-oriented, not masochistic, and above all, not afraid. For in saying "exhort the free" she is suggesting that the free have a tendency to soft and flabby living—I do not know if the free entertained themselves with Atari games in her day or what the equivalent in trivialization of life might have been. Perhaps exhorting the free, waking the well up to their own moral and personal responsibilities is a harder task than caring for the sick. Fundamentalism is sentimental: It never allows the individual his or her room for growth, development of talent and spiritual work. But Mechtild is not fundamentalist: She settles the works vs. faith dispute with a single sentence: "Half of our good and virtuous activity is a gift from God" she declares, and "half belongs to ourselves." Mechtild is a worker, not a complainer, not a person without hope.

3. Let us praise Mechtild for being an awakened individual, a conscious individual, a critical individual. She is truly radical in the sense of root-oriented for she criticizes herself and her own commitments. For example, although she loved Christianity and stayed within it, she criticizes some of its priests calling them

"foolish layfolk" who never accept their own responsibility for renewing the church. Though she was herself a Beguine she actually criticizes the Beguines! This is the difference between a liberal and a radical: A liberal tells others what is wrong with them; a radical is able to criticize his or her own home, own institution, own self and lifestyles as well as others. Mechtild was radical. I believe that such prophetic criticism is sorely needed in society and in church life today. Churches have come a long way in the past twenty years in developing social conscience and justice awareness vis-a-vis society's gross social sins. But regarding injustice within churches themselves, the silence speaks louder than either words or actions. Mechtild would not hesitate to speak to this issue.

4. Let us praise Mechtild for her acute consciousness of the suffering of her own people, namely of women and of the poor. Regarding the latter she stresses how Joseph was poor and how both he and Mary made their living by their hands—the way Beguines themselves made a living. Regarding the former, she points out how no one of Jesus' close friends stuck by him at the cross except "one woman, his mother." In a vision she had of hell she says not a single woman was there except "princesses who with their princes loved all kinds of sin." She tells the nuns she lived with in her final years to "preach boldly" and she speaks of her own masculine side that she had to develop in order to write and publish her book. In this way she reveals that she is not projecting her masculinity onto "the perfect" husband or father or prelate but is taking responsibility for developing both the feminine and masculine sides of her self. Time and again she strikes out at temptations to masochism or the putting-down-of-oneself, what psychologist Karen Horney calles "I can't ism", that a sadistic culture wants to teach its poor and its oppressed. "How wonderful my soul is," she declares. In this regard she is very conscious of the word "power" and she works to redefine it. "I rise up with power" she says—here is the end of masochism, the beginning of the end of sadism, and the origins of authentic relationships of mutuality. I have the power, she declares "to change my ways." The power of transformation is the ultimate meaning of power for Mechtild. And this transformation, which we all need to undergo in our lives, also applies to society. It is very different from the power of crusade or of clericalism or of other sexual or racial privilege.

5. Let us praise Mechtild for loving a God who is not a stoic, impassable, unmoved Mover of a God. Mechtild's God is

vulnerable both to pleasure and to pain. God gives joy and God receives joy. God undergoes pain and God rejoices when pain is relieved. God's Son dances with us and we with God. Celebration, indeed circle-dancing as in what we today call "Sara's Circle," is sung about by Mechtild. "You shall dance merrily," God instructs her: "Leap in ordered dance." And the dance will lead to prophetic action: "Be a vanquisher of evil spirits!" If God is a vulnerable God, then humans too are to be vulnerable and in touch with their deep vulnerability. If God is a pleasurable God, then humans too are invited to pleasurable living and shared, estatic living. If God is a suffering God, then humans too are invited to get in touch with their own and others' pain. Only from this depth will compassion be born. Here lies the ultimate transformation for Mechtild: The transforming of us into compassionate instruments of the Holy Spirit. For in Mechtild's theology the Holy Spirit "is a compassionate out-pouring of the Creator and the Son."

6. Let us praise Mechtild for her genius in birthing images of humanity's deepest journeys. Mechtild was in close touch with her right brain—but never at the expense of the left brain. About the latter she insists, "love without knowledge is darkness to the wise person." And so she insists on balancing love with knowledge, right brain with left. But her right brain was so deeply fertile—it was precisely here in her imagery that she has most profoundly influenced western culture through two men who read her and drank deeply of her images and of the feminist images that she herself represented: namely, Dante and Meister Eckhart. Dante owes much to Mechtild and the tradition she represents for her images of spiritual journey, sinking, spiraling.

But it is especially the great Rhineland mystic Meister Eckhart (1260-1329) who owes the greatest debt to Mechtild of Magdeburg. Both Mechtild and Eckhart were born and grew up in the German province of Thuringia. Eckhart became a Dominican and it should be noted that Mechtild was related intimately to the Dominican spiritual movement all of her adult life. She reminds us on several occasions that Dominic was her favorite saint and that Dominicans—many of whom were chaplains to the Beguines—are her companions in her struggle. Heinrich of Halle was a Dominican who became her confidant and spiritual director and actually got her book published and translated in her lifetime so that many could read it. Heinrich was in fact a student of St. Albert the Great, the famed teacher of both Thomas Aquinas and, in his last year, Meister Eckhart. There can be no question, therefore, that

Mechtild's book was circulating widely in Dominican circles in Eckhart's day. Mechtild obviously knew Thomas Aquinas' work as taught her by the Dominicans.

In her Introduction Sue Woodruff shows some excellent parallels between Mechtild's and Eckhart's naming of the spiritual journey. I would like to draw attention to some images shared by Mechtild and Eckhart. The very title of the book, "The Flowing Light of the Godhead" is significant since *flowing* is one of Eckhart's as well as Mechtild's most recurring images. We flow into God and God into us they both say. The title "Godhead" for God is important to Eckhart as it was to Mechtild. Mechtild acknowledges humanity's divinity and divinization with the image of God's divinity flowing into us. Eckhart follows suit. Instead of conceiving of spiritual disciplines in terms of exercises of climbing up ladders, Mechtild invokes the gentler image of "sinking." So does Eckhart. Mechtild talks often of God as "fire" and of the "crackling of God" within and without us. This image evokes Eckhart's use of the "inner spark" in each person, the source of creativity and the Holy Spirit. Mechtild, like Eckhart, talks of our "melting" with divine life, of "bubbling over," of remaining young in the sense of "ever fresh and ever green," of returning to "the Source." All these images are ripe and rich in Eckhart as well. Mechtild invokes the fish and hook image, complaining of having been hooked on God; Eckhart tells a similar story. While Mechtild can talk about herself as male, Eckhart talks of himself as pregnant like a woman with child. Both Mechtild and Eckhart distrust asceticism but instead counsel "being still", "being quiet" and loving nothingness and darkness. Both invoke images of God as an underground river that floods over and springs up into the person who is "bare to himself or herself." The emptying images of the via negativa are important to both. Both find the culmination of the spiritual journey not in a contemplative gazing at but in creativity and bearing fruit. We are to move "from knowledge to fruition and fruitfulness and beyond," counsels Mechtild. Yes, "we will have a creative kingdom." And both counsel celebration of God's gifts and the directing of creativity toward relief of our neighbor's suffering in compassion. True emptying, an authentic via negativa, leads to creative service, pouring out of compassion. And both Mechtild and Eckhart are fond of circle imagery—"there," Mechtild writes, "will I remain and circle evermore." Both are panentheists—we are in God and God in us. Thus both have overcome the religious dualism implicit in all theism—i.e. the notion that God is exclusively "out there" and in all introverted spiritualities which see God only "inside."

In all these parallels between Mechtild and Eckhart it should be stressed that Eckhart read Mechtild but Mechtild did not read Eckhart. For Mechtild died when Eckhart was about twenty years old. Therefore it must be stressed that it is Eckhart who is in debt to Mechtild and the Beguine movement which was the women's movement of his day. Mechtild's trust of her images led to her persecution and her making many enemies in a corrupt church. So did Eckhart's. While Mechtild was never condemned as such, the Beguine movement was condemned and by the same Pope who condemned Meister Eckhart. Mechtild in fact became a third order Dominican—as did many Beguines—when the Beguines were initially condemned (though they were later allowed to reconstitute themselves so long as they were not "transient" in their lifestyles). It can be said, then, that both Eckhart and Mechtild paid a price for trusting their images. The price of the prophet who is also a mystic.

We need prophets like this today in society and all its institutions including the church ones. And we will only have them if we also have mystics—persons who have learned to live lifestyles that witness against culture's suppositions; who are in touch with feeling but avoid sentimentalism and thus make passion lead to actions of compassion; who are critical and self-critical including of one's own institutions as regards injustice; who are in touch with people's suffering, including one's own; who can celebrate a pleasure-loving as well as a suffering God and who themselves know both pleasure and pain; who trust their images and live out their right brain experience and share it with others. Thank you, Mechtild, for the timely prophetic mysticism you bring to us in this book. Thank you, Sue Woodruff, for making Mechtild available again. And thank you, Meister Eckhart, for learning from such courageous and imaginative women as Mechtild of Magdeburg. May we who live in the human race's most violent century do no less.

Matthew Fox, op
Institute of Creation-Centered
Spirituality
Mundelein College
Chicago

Introduction

I met an older sister during summer school last year. She was about seventy years old, blind and in poor health. She had left her home in Magdeburg a few years previously. Because of her outspoken criticism of the local clergy, they encouraged her to get out of town. Enchanted by this fascinating woman, I invited her home for the weekend. She agreed to come and to tell me her story. We sat in the shade of a tree in our backyard on a bluff overlooking the slough and facing Mt. Tamalpais, talking and drinking in the peace.

Mechtild was born about 1210 in a small town on the Elbe River in what is now East Germany. As a young girl of twelve, she first felt the call of the Holy Spirit. In fact she speaks of herself as God's "Playmate." (iv,3)[1] "Your childhood was a companion of my Holy Spirit." (vii,3) He has taken her to secret places where "God alone will play with (her) in a game of which the body knows nothing." (i,2) God leads "the child in you in wonderful ways." (i,25)

As she grew up Mechtild enjoyed the rich courtly scene of medieval society. The dances, the beautiful women, the handsome youths, the royalty, all left vivid images on the impressionable young girl. As she matured inwardly, she used this imagery to paint her relationship with the Lord. A good example is the courtly dance described on page 50. Around Mechtild swirl images of her young life. From them she leaps joyfully into the circle of love. Her dream/visions abound with graphic descriptions of the white robes of the maidens, of their rose-colored cloaks, of a hat of peacock feathers worn by the Bride of Christ, of the handsome young men bearing gifts of roses, bouquets of lilies, and nosegays of violets. She easily translates images of crowns, princes, banners and pageantry into the language of her soul.

As we sipped lemonade in the California sun, Mechtild recounted her decision to leave her home, her family, and this sumptuous life. At the age of twenty-three sne felt a call to remove herself from the courtly scene. So off she went to the big city, Magdeburg. She only knew a few people there and deliberately chose to live apart from them. A single woman, she aligned herself with the Beguines[2], a loosely structured group of lay women who worked among the sick in the city. She called her new life "The Desert" in contrast to her former existence. In the poem on page 73 Mechtild outlines her ideals as a young woman.

Through the Beguines, Mechtild said she met the Dominicans. She laughed and asked if I knew that the Dominicans were called the "Domini Canes," Dogs of God. Often she refers to herself as such. "God showed this to a lame dog who, with lamentations, was still licking its wounds." (ii,20) Mechtild takes seriously for herself and her fellow Dominicans the role of faithful, alert watchdogs. She prays for "the gift every dog has by nature, that of being true to her master." (ii,25) In Hebrew the word for prophet also indicates a barking dog. Mechtild follows this lead as she likens her prayer and counsel to a dog's barking. "What use is it that the dog barks? While the owner sleeps the thief breaks into the house! But our efforts sometimes awaken such sleeping sinners." (vii,3) Mechtild had a prophetic vision and she knew it.

Through this contact with the Dominicans, Mechtild met Heinrich from Halle, a town a short distance from Magdeburg. He became her spiritual director. She shared herself with him showing him her poems, notes, and visions. At his insistence Mechtild began to jot these prayers and thoughts on paper and send them to him. Heinrich collected the pieces into six books. He expressed a bit of concern about her style prompting this reply from Mechtild: "Master Heinrich! You are surprised at the masculine way in which this book is written? I wonder why that surprises you?" (v,12)

Hearing again of this book and intrigued by her comments, I asked Mechtild if she would let me read it. She said Yes — on one condition: "You shall read it nine times, faithfully, humbly, and devoutly." (i, introduction) I found that quite a challenge for a short summer encounter. But she reiterated, "All who would understand this book should read it nine times." (i,introduction)

So I settled myself the next week to this monumental task. Remembering Matthew Fox's presentation on images of the soul in Eckhart's writings,[3] I thought to ask Mechtild if she had written much about the soul. Her response: "I ponder much and reflect in my human senses how wonderful my soul is." (v,26)

Once I had read Mechtild's seven books straight through, I went back to each one separately and read it a second time, taking time to relish and reflect. For my third reading I took notes on the images she used for the soul and for God. The soul for Mechtild was most certainly an image of God. So much so that an image used on one page to indicate God might crop up again on the next to depict the soul.

SOUL	GOD
a living spark (i, 28)	a little spark (vi,13)
Love's prisoner (i,28)	I, God, am imprisoned (ii,25)
Soaring like an eagle (i,38)	O soaring eagle (ii,3)
O glorious sun (i,18)	my sun! (i,4)
a cooling stream (i,19)	My flowing stream! (i,4)
a healing ointment (ii,9)	a healing salve (ii,10)
I would ever be your physician! (iii,2)	God must be my physician (vii,58)
You clothe yourself with my soul	who yourself are its cloak (ii,5)
Now have I sung you	if only you would sing me (ii,5)

My fourth reading of Mechtild consisted of organizing the images of the soul that appeared in her books. I grouped some of her images, especially the dominant, repetitive or unusual ones. For my fifth and sixth readings, I became involved in a different extrovert meditation. I lettered each group of images together on one page. I selected drawings and paintings I had done that summer to accompany each page of the manuscript. These I then assembled in a book form. In this book I share these images with you, the reader.

Mechtild has a sense of humor concerning her images. She grows old gracefully with a gentle laughing look at herself. She touches on themes as old as the book of Job, the Psalms, the Song of Songs. Her writings abound in images of light, fire, reflection, love, longing. She sees the soul in these

13

images and God in the same images. We are the spark; God is the fire. We are the fire; God is the light. We are the light; God is the moon. We are the moon; God is the sun. We are the sun; God is love. We are love; God is compassion. We are compassionate; we resemble God.

In her vision of the soul in God and God in the soul, Mechtild foreshadows the panentheism found in the writings of Meister Eckhart. There is a clear, almost diaphanous, quality in the flow of light in and through her life and in this too she resembles Eckhart—or does Eckhart resemble her? In fact the only extant manuscript (MS No 277) of Mechtild's writings are found bound with some sermons of Meister Eckhart in the library of Einsiedeln. Meister Eckhart, being some fifty years her junior and being a Dominican from Hochheim, must have known of Mechtild and her work. She wrote for Heinrich, her spiritual director, and for us the journal of her soul's growth and flowering. Eckhart drew for us a portrait of this same process.

The spiritual quest begins with an awakening of the soul, spirals through experiences of nothingness and emptiness and culminated in a personal rebirthing of oneself and of one's God in oneself. This overflows in a profound sense of compassion, an integration of one's spiritual and social consciousness and activity.

Eckhart and Mechtild chronical the mystical identification of the soul with creation and the Creator. The soul awakens to a new awareness of the splendor of this world, of nature, of herself, of the universe and of the Power which brought all this to life. The soul shines in the blessing that is creation. Says Mechtild: God comes to the soul as "dew on the flowers," (i,13) and in "the song of the birds!" (i,44) "All creatures bear the imprint of God's nature," reminds Eckhart.[4] God "has given Himself with all creatures wholly to me," (ii,23) says Mechtild. Her prayer response: "I bless you without ceasing in my heart for all earthly things." (v,21) Our mouth she tells us is "to praise God with inconceivable praise in common with all creatures, with all our doings at all times." (iv,18)

For Mechtild as for Eckhart the soul must love the Creator in the creatures of this world. (vi,4) "God loved us from the beginning," (vii,55) for the "Holy Trinity gave itself in the creation of all things and made us body and soul in infinite

14

love. We were fashioned most nobly." (iii,9) In Eckhart's words, "God was pregnant with every creature from all eternity." (91)

Both of these medieval mystics reject the dualism that splits soul from body. Ecstasy involves the whole human person. "And you shall evermore soar and delight soul and body in My Holy Trinity, immersed as a fish in the sea." (v,25) Eckhart cautions us not to conclude that the soul alone "does this or that; rather one should say: I do this or recognize that, because body and soul are one." (116) Keeping this body/soul unity in mind, Mechtild listens to the word of God spoken in her heart. "I can never be sundered from you. However far we be parted never can we be separated." (ii,25) Eckhart too recognizes the action of God. "Because God gives himself, the soul is immersed in him, it lives in him." (117)

For Mechtild "the soul is a god with God." (vi,1) To her God speaks: "I am the God of all gods; you art the goddess of all creatures." (iii,9) "The seed of God," Eckhart says, "is in us." (188) Just as pear seeds grow into pear trees and hazel seeds into hazel trees, so too grows "the seed of God into God." (118) Thus Mechtild advises one of her sisters "Make your heart crystal clear within." (v,11) This God-life lives in us as a seed, a spark of fire, a gleam of light, a flood of love. "Great is the overflow of Divine Love for it is never still. Always ceaselessly and tirelessly it pours itself out, so that the small vessel which is ourselves might be filled to the brim and might also overflow." (vii,55)

These two great German friends of God call us to an awareness of and identification with creation and the Creator. We—body, soul, male, female, young, old—mirror the splendor of creation. We are the ground, the humus, where the God-seed can germinate, root and flower forth in our day. But a seed bed is dark. For a long time nothing seems to be happening. The earth seems dry and lifeless. An emptiness and suffering washes over our human lives always leaving questions.

Mechtild acknowledges that the gift of her writing was given to her at first tenderly, then secretly and "now with much suffering." (vi,20) She reveals her experience: "Then the soul and body came into such a gross darkness that I lost light and

15

consciousness and knew no more of God's intimacy." (iv,12) She knows that "when the light in the lantern burns out the beauty of the lantern can no longer be seen." (vii,27) Often at night she prays with "longing and distress because of (her) nothingness." (vii,14) She perceives that it is love, not strength of will or determination, which opens her to God's presence. "Those who would storm the heights by fierceness and ascetic practices deceive themselves badly. Such people carry grim hearts within themselves, they lack true humility which alone leads the soul to God." (ii,1)

The truly humble person, the one in touch with the earth (*humus*) knows how "to live now in bare freedom and complete emptiness, having no need to possess or acquire anything whether little or much. For everything belonging to God belongs to them." (167) "The ground of the soul," Eckhart says, "is dark." (174)

Mechtild images sin as a high mountain that puts darkness and distance between herself and God. (iv,5) She suffers much in her lifetime. She endures the pain of many illnesses. She suffers anguish when she perceives God hiding from her. "How bitter to me, when you shun me!" (ii,25) She feels powerless at her inability to bring to fruition all the good she desires. (vi,19) She is assaulted by peace-breakers, people who distort the good things she has done and who steal her honour as much as possible by their words. (iv,2) She laments: "Oh Lord! how long must I remain here on earth in this mortal body as a target at which people throw stones and shoot and assail my honor with their evil cunning?" (vi,38) She chafes at the strictures of her aging body. "Our childhood was foolish, our youth troubled. Alas! Now, in my old age I find much to criticize, for it can produce no shining works; it can be cold and without grace. Life appears powerless now that it no longer has youth to help it endure the fiery love of God. It is impatient—little ills afflict it much which in youth it noticed hardly at all. Yes, a good old age must be full of patient waiting and trust in God alone." (vii,3) Finally she "can no longer bear her loneliness; she must share it with all the friends of God." (vii,31) To her sisters she cries: "Suffer? I too suffer!" (vi,1) From her trials Mechtild learns the ageless wisdom of a dialectical psychology: embracing one's pain is essential to becoming whole again. "Whoever is sore wounded by love

16

will never be made whole unless she embrace tne very same love which wounded her." (ii,15)

Mechtild understood early the emptiness, the barrenness from which new life comes.

You shall love the nothing,
flee the self.
Stand alone.
Seek help from no one.
Let your being be quiet,
Be free from the bondage of all things.

Eckhart also acknowledges the need for solitude. "The true Word of eternity will be spoken only in solitude, where people are made desolate and estranged from themselves." (240) This emptiness exerts a profound influence. "For if something empty existed under heaven, no matter what you wish and no matter whether it be large or small, (God) would either carry it up to himself in heaven or have to come down and fill it with himself. (242) The purpose of emptiness is to receive, to be filled. Suffering is not for one's own sake; "this suffering will hurt you and will be hard to carry. If you are suffering for God and for his sake, the suffering will not hurt you and will also not be hard for you because God will be carrying the burden." (276)

Both Mechtild and Eckhart call us to an awareness of the poverty, pain and emptiness that exist in our lives, but they do not in any way encourage our bathing in misery. Darkness becomes a "rich sensitivity in which you will be made whole. For this reason there is positively no turning back." (240) Out of the darkness light is born. Eckhart begs us to pay attention to this birth within ourselves. "Wait only for this birth within yourself, and you will discover all blessing and all consolation, all bliss, all being, and all truth." (251) We are called to a new sense of ourselves, a new awareness of our world and a new relationship with our God. We are open to being changed and to changing our universe.

Love transforms. "Love makes empty hearts overflow. This happens even more when we have to struggle through without assurance, all unready for the play of Love." (iv,19) To the empty soul, unready but open, is given "the true blessing of God which flows from the heavenly flood out of

17

the spring of the flowing Trinity. This flowing contains such power that it takes all strength from the body and lays the soul naked to itself." (i,2) Mechtild, experiencing the flow of God within herself, begins to "ponder much and reflect in (her) human senses how wonderful (her) soul is." (vi,26)

New life surges through her. "God has given her the power to change her ways." (vi,7) In her open heart "one finds Truth and Discretion in all things." (v,11) This awakening love quiets her movements; she becomes "outwardly still, for outward activity hinders the inward working of the spirit." (vii,34) As Eckhart reminds us, "God needs nothing more than for us to offer him a quiet heart." (381) At the same time, "the soul would never come to rest unless God brought himself into the soul and the soul into God." (366)

But this does not mean nothing is happening. For "wherever genius combines wisdom and love, there creation bears fruit." (v,28) Enthusiastically Mechtild puts her heart into all her work participating in a new creation of herself, of God in her. "I come soaring like an eagle swinging myself from the depths up into the heights." (i,38) "There," she says, "will I remain and circle evermore." (i,44) Eckhart calls this heaven. "Heaven runs constantly in a circle; therefore it has to be round so that it can run more swiftly in a circle." (367) Here is the birthplace of the child who is ourself and the child who is God in us. "When you reach the point where you cannot feel sorrow or anxiety over everything, and where sorrow is not sorrow for you, and where all things are a pure kind of peace for you then a child is really born." (330)

Yes, God is born again in us. Christmas and Easter happen in us. "When your Easter comes, I shall be all around you. I shall be through and through you, and I shall steal your body and give you to your Love." (i,3) Then "God lays the soul in his glowing heart so that He, the great God, and she, the humble maid, embrace and are united as thoroughly as water is with wine." (i,4) In Eckhart's words, "As true as it is that God became a human, so true is it that humans became God." (359) A birth of God does take place in us. "As love grows and expands in the soul, it rises eagerly to God and overflows towards the Glory which bends towards it. Then Love melts through the soul into the senses, so that the body too might share in it, for Love is drawn into all things." (v,4) Mechtild

18

urges us to "make our souls a cradle and lay the Beloved there with joyful and loving hearts offering Him praise and glory." (vii,21)[5]

Eckhart sees that "quite the same way, however as God breaks through me, I shall breakthrough him in return! God leads this spirit into the desert and solitude of himself where he is pure unity and gushes up only within himself. This spirit no longer has a why." (355) Through this birth Mechtild now can say, "Fly, dove-winged one, and soar in all things beyond yourself. But then when you are wearied return to the flood again." (vii,25) For "I have lost myself in You," (iii,1) she cries. "Great love does not flow with tears. Rather it burns in the great Fire of Heaven. In this Fire it flows and flows swiftly yet remains in itself in a very great stillness. (iv,16) "Silence and quietness must reign there," cautions Eckhart, "and the Father must speak and generate his Son and accomplish his deeds there without any images." He promises, "Lay hold of God in all things and this will be a sign of your birth, a sign that God has given birth in you himself as his only begotten Son, and nothing less." (67) As Mechtild claims, "God is my parent by nature." (vi,31) She hears the Spirit speak to the Father: "We will no longer be unfruitful! We will have a creative kingdom." (iii,9)

Mechtild sees God as a mother who "lifts her loved child from the ground to her knee." (iv,22) She finds her soul in the Trinity which is like "a mother's cloak wherein the child finds a home and lays its head on the maternal breast." (vi,7) Eckhart too speaks of God as mother, birther, Creator.

Both Eckhart and Mechtild invite us to an awareness of these births: the birth of a new self, the birth of God in ourselves, the birth of ourselves as daughters and sons of a God who is both Mother and Father. We are called to participate in the "creative kingdom" (iii,9) We are called to give new life to our world, to transform it. This is a birthing call. "Life means a sort of overflow by which a thing, welling up within itself, completely floods itself, each part of it interpenetrating every other part, until at last it pours itself out and boils over into something external." (204) This outpouring is the spilling over of compassion through our lives. "When we on earth pour out compassion and mercy from the depths of our hearts and give to the poor and dedicate our bodies to the service of the broken, to that very extent do we resemble the Holy Spirit who is a compassionate out-pouring of the Creator and the Son." (vi,32)

Eckhart points out that we are "compassionate like the Father when we are compassionate, not from passion, not from impulse, but from deliberate choice and reasonable decision." (424) Mechtild sees virtues as "half a gift from God, half belongs to ourselves." (vi,30) We must use the gifts; "we can and we ought to make use of everything that comes our way." (vi,42) God is ever generous in the outpouring of gifts to us. (i,17) The gift of compassion Eckhart notes "directs a person to relationships with her fellow human beings." (421) "God's peace prompts fraternal service, so that one creature sustains the other. One is enriching the other, that is why all creatures are interdependent." (446) Mechtild prays to be "ever constant in your service." (vii,19) She pleads with compassion: "stay by me that I may diligently serve the broken and bear the cost of such service in my goods and in my body." (vii,48)

She loves her friends and recognizes that she can be a help to them. (iii,21) She realizes with Eckhart that "there have never been saints whom sorrow did not grieve and love did not please and there never will be such saints." (485) Mechtild also knows that her friends will not always understand her or the life she chooses. (iii,3) Like Eckhart, Mechtild understands "you should know and you should have considered to what vocation you are most strongly called by God. For all people are not called to God in one way." (475) Early in her life she hears the call: "you shall loose those who are bound, you shall exhort the free. You shall care for the broken yet in all this you shall dwell alone." (i,35) She seeks to grow in wisdom and spread it abroad for others. (vi,32) She labors swiftly with her hands. (vi,12) She strives to "bear adversity with love." (iv,1) She values faithfulness in friendship. (v,22) She lives "welcoming to all." (ii,21)

Driven from town to town by her political foes, Mechtild arrives late in life at the convent at Helfde in Saxony where she seeks to "enlighten and teach." (vii,8) She calls on the sisters to "compassionately do good to such as they know need it." (vii,5) Being chosen superior does not place her in a position of power over her sisters. "Power is made for service. I am your servant; I am not your master." (vi,1) Mechtild lived out the advice of Eckhart: "Take nothing into account except the need and necessity of this

20

other person." (535) As superior she goes daily to the sick-house to "heal the broken with the comforting words of God, cheer them gently with earthly joys." (vi,1) She encourages the sisters to "cherish cleanliness in the sick," to "be merry and laugh with them," and to "carry their secret needs in the deepest silence of your heart." (vi,1)

She also visits the guest house daily to give all the help she can to the young people staying there, acting "according to the loving-kindness of God." (vi,1) Finally she is off to the kitchen to make sure the day's food and drink is tasty and plentiful. Singing, prayer and study require a certain refreshment. (vi,1) With Eckhart, Mechtild wishes us to "understand that bread is given to us that not only we might eat but that we recognize others in need, lest anyone say 'my bread' is given to me instead of understanding that it is ours, given to me, to others through me and to me through others." (499) Mechtild summons herself to be "lovingly cheerful or deeply earnest with (her sisters); compassionate regarding their work, sending them forth with loving words, preaching boldly." (vi,1) She challenges them: "Do not judge others. Stand by them with love. Then God will lead them to be open with you." (vi,1)

Compassion as a way of life, of transforming this world, is preached and practiced by Mechtild. "Each of us who seeks compassion and calls upon compassion resolutely conquers the sorrow and depression that lives in our hearts. Compassion lays her gentle hand on what is broken. She comforts the sad, heals the wounds and lifts the hearts of all who come to her." (vii,62) "In so far as we love compassion and practice it steadfastly, to that extent do we resemble the heavenly Creator who practices these things ceaselessly in us." (vi,32) Throughout the writings of Mechtild and Eckhart we find an outpouring of compassion. Their vision of the transforming power of love flows from their journey along a spiraling path which brings them ever closer to the Creator. The soul awakens to the blessing that is creation finding its rightful place therein. Pain and emptiness are the depths from which a new life, a new consciousness, emerges. Death again gives birth to life. This energy impels a transformation of the world, a compassionate concern for people that spills over onto all creation.

After all of this, I realised that I still had three readings to reach Mechtild's mystical nine! Along the way in my note-taking I kept a separate listing of favorite poems and one liners that really did not necessarily contribute to the image of soul or the illustration of the spiritual journey. Yet I was like "the fish (that) looks eagerly at the red fly with which the fisherman will take him; but it does not see the hook." (vii,27) So I was hooked into some more lettering! This time I chose separate papers for each saying. When I completed the lettering I read them each again and added some lines of paint that flowed from this reading (my eighth!). I invite you to read her words quoted in this book a second time; choose one phrase, line or poem. Take a plain piece of paper and letter or write her words carefully, meditatively with a colored marking pen. Then using simple water colors brush on a line or two of your favorite colors. Do it with love. Enjoy your extrovert meditation. This is how I read Mechtild's words the eighth time.

Before I completed the mystical ninth reading, I wanted to visit this wonderfully wise woman again. So I invited her to the beach. We went with another friend of mine. But the beach was fogged in so we stopped near a pond. I knew Mechtild had been ill much of her adult life. In fact for the last thirty years she had expected to die momentarily. I had heard that she feared death. I asked her now that she is nearing the end of her life what images help her to cope with approaching death. One, she said, was a sea image. Not crashing waves, but "the rippling tide of love which flows secretly out from God into the soul and draws it mightily back into its Source." (vi,189) A gently moving God who reaches out daily to her gathers her up at last in a flow of love to carry her powerfully back to Herself. In another image she finds helpful, Mechtild hears God explain "I will draw my breath and your soul shall come to Me as a needle to a magnet." (v,158) God breathes out and we live. God breathes in and we home to Her as a needle is drawn strongly, mysteriously to a magnet.

Just as the earlier poem about the desert drew a picture of the life chosen by the younger woman, this poem portrays the living out of that life by a mature Mechtild.

> Do you wish to know my meaning?
> Then lie down in the Fire.
> See and taste the Flowing
> Godhead through your being;
> Feel the Holy Spirit
> Moving and compelling
> You within the Flowing
> Fire and Light of God. (vi,29)

These last lines bring us back to the beginning of Mechtild's book: *The Flowing Light of the Godhead*. God is not static, out there, uninvolved. God flows into us and we into God.

I wish to thank Mechtild for the time she spent with me sharing her wisdom and her life. This communication would never have occurred without the translation of Mechtild's words by Lucy Menzies, a translation on which my versions depend. I am grateful to Matt Fox for introducing me to Mechtild and for his patient support during the birth of this book. Thanks to Noel for taking us to the pond; to Joe for releasing the magic of paint; to the Sisters in Marin who shared their yard with us.

Sue Woodruff

NOTES

[1]Each entry from Mechtild's writings has two reference numbers. The first, a Roman numeral, indicates one of her seven 'books' which constitute for one volume. The second number indicates the entry number given in *The Revelation of Mechtild of Magdeburg* or *The Flowing Light of the Godhead*, trans. Lucy Menzies (London: Longmans, Green and Co., 1953).

[2]For a fuller discussion of the Beguines and their masculine counterpart, the Beghards, cf. Ernest W. McDonnell, *The Beguines and Beghards in Medieval Culture* (New Brunswick, New Jersey: Rutgers University Press, 1954).

[3]Cf. Matthew Fox, O.P., "Searching for the Authentically Human: Images of Soul in Meister Eckhart and Teresa of Avila," in *Dimensions of Contemporary Spirituality*, ed. Francis A. Eigo, O.S.A., Proceedings of the Theology Institute of Villanova University (Villanova, Pennsylvania: Villanova University Press, 1982). pp. 1-39.

[4]Single numbers in parentheses are page numbers for quotations of Eckhart's writings taken from Matthew Fox, O.P., *Breakthrough: Meister Eckhart's Creation Spirituality in New Translation* (Garden City, New York: Doubleday and Co.,1980).

[5]Cradles were often kept in churches in Bavaria. Women who wished to become mothers would come and rock them. The cradles were part of the furniture used for the Nativity celebration. Cf. Lina Eckenstein, *Woman Under Monasticism* (Cambridge: University Press, 1896).

23

I. ORIGINS:

DELIGHTING

I ponder much
and reflect in my human senses
how wonderful
my soul is!

You speak to me of my beginnings?
I will tell you.

I was created in love.

For that reason
nothing can express my beauty
nor liberate my nobleness
except love alone.

God

    did not create the human race

        for adversity.

    But for love.

God

    created the human person

        from the necessity

            of love.

You ask me where God dwells.

I will tell you.
      There is no lord in the whole world
            who lives in all his dwellings at once
      except
            God alone.

God says:

> Now is the time
> to tell you where I am
> and where I will be.

> I am

> > in Myself,
> > in all places
> > in all things
> > as I ever have been
> without beginning.

God,

    You are the sun,

        I am your reflection.

        When God shines
          we must
            reflect.

In heaven, our origin,
     before each soul and body
     therein gleamed the reflection of the Holy
Trinity.
From the mirror
     there shone the sublime reflection of each
person
     in the high majesty from which it had flowed
forth.
     Each of us is a mirror
        of eternal contemplation, with a
     reflection that must surely be that
     of the living Son of God
     with all his works.

What is the human soul?

       The soul is a god with God.

This is why God says to the soul:
       I am the God of all gods;
       but you are the goddess of all creatures.

     Stand in fatherly fashion
       by all people who bear my likeness.
       For I am

         your soul.

From the very beginning
    God loved us.
The Holy Trinity
    gave itself
    in the creation of all things
and made us,
body and soul,
in infinite love.
We were fashioned most nobly.

God takes such delight in the human person
that Divinity sings this song to our soul:

> O lovely rose on the thorn!
> O hovering bee in the honey!
> O pure dove in your being!
> O glorious sun in your setting!
> O full moon in your course!
>> From you
>>> I your God
>>>> will never
>>> turn away.

How does God come to us?
    Like
        dew on the flowers
    Like
        the song of the birds!

    Yes, God gives himself
        with all creatures
        wholly
            to me.

Love flows

> **from God**
> > **to humans**
> **without effort:**
> **As a bird**
> > **glides through the air**
> > **without moving its wings —**
> **Thus they go**
> > **wherever they wish**
> > **united in body and soul**
> **Yet separate in form.**

Fish cannot drown in the water,
Birds cannot sink in the air,
Gold cannot perish
    in the refiner's fire.
This God gives to all creatures:
To develop and seek their own nature —
How then can I withstand mine?
    I must
        to God,
            My Parent through nature,
            My Brother through humanity,
            My Spouse through love,
        God's am I for ever.

The truly wise person

    kneels

        at the feet of all creatures
and is not afraid to endure
    the mockery of others.

The manifold delight
> I learn to take in earthly things
> can never drive me
>> from my love.
For,
> in the nobility of creatures,
> in their beauty
> and in their usefulness,
I will love God —
and not myself!

This is why I bless God in my heart
without ceasing
for every earthly thing.

And this is why God gave us a mouth —

to praise God
with inconceivable praise
in common with all creatures
with all our doings
at all times.

The day of my spiritual awakening
was the day I saw
and knew I saw
all things in God
and God
in all things.

Do not disdain your body.
    For the soul
        is just as safe in its body
            as in the Kingdom of Heaven —
            though not so certain.
        It is just as daring —
            but not so strong,
        just as powerful —
            but not so constant,
        just as loving —
            but not so joyful,
        just as gentle —
            but not so rich,
        just as holy —
            but not yet so sinless,
        just as content —
            but not so complete.

We ought to imprint

all God's gifts

into our hearts.

O, soul, you are perfect —
        Rejoice!
    For you alone are like God.

Come racing like a hunted deer.
    For you are the image of my Divine Godhead.
    You are a foundation of my Divine Being.
This is why
    the pure lamb
        laid itself on its own image
        in the stall of your body.

I who am Divine
    am truly in you.

    I can never be sundered from you;
    However far we be parted
    Never can we be separated.

I am in you
    and you are in Me,
We could not be any closer.
We two are fused into one,
Poured into a single mould,
Thus, unwearied,
    we shall remain forever.

I, God, am your playmate!
    I will lead the child in you
    in wonderful ways
    for I have chosen you.

Beloved child, come swiftly to Me
    For I am truly in you.

Remember this:
    The smallest soul of all
    is still the daughter of the Father,
        the sister of the Son,
            the friend of the Holy Spirit
    and the true bride of the Holy Trinity.

Woman,
  you must adorn yourself!
Maiden,
  you ought to dance merrily
  dance like my elected one!
Dance like
  the noblest,
      loveliest,
        richest Queen!
And,
    if you meet Me with the flowering desire
      of flowing love,
    then must I touch you
      with my Divine nature as my Queen.

  Then
  you shall soar forever
  and delight — soul and body —
  in my Holy Trinity,
  immersed like a fish in the sea.
For the fish
    cannot live long
      stranded on the shore.

When,
    Oh when will you soar
        on the wings of your longing
        to the blissful heights?

I cannot dance, O Lord,
    unless you lead me.
        If you will
    that I leap joyfully
    then you must be the first to dance
        and to sing!

Then, and only then,
    will I leap for love.

Then will I soar
        from love to knowledge,
        from knowledge to fruition
        from fruition to beyond
            all human sense.

And there
        I will remain
        and circle for evermore.

O full moon in your course!

O glorious sun in your shining!

I am a bride clothed by the sun
and I tread the moon under my feet.

Sisters and brothers, listen.
Make your heart crystal clear within.
Your senses will be opened
and your soul so transparent
that we will see
into
the wisdom
of God.

God says:

    My dove,
    in your sighings
    I soar in you.
    You unspotted dove!
    Welcome, sweet dove.
    Soar on wings of your longing.

My body

    soars
        in a supernatural peace
    And I shall evermore
    soar and delight
    soul and body
        in my Holy Trinity.

God leads the child he has called in wonderful ways.
    God takes the soul
    to a secret place,
    for God alone will play with it
    in a game of which the body knows nothing

God says: "I am your playmate!
    Your childhood was a companion
        of my Holy Spirit."

Come, Love!
    Sing on
    let me hear you sing this song!
    Sing for joy
    and laugh
    for I the Creator
        am truly subject
            to all creatures.

God has enough of all good things
except one:
Of communion with humans
God can never have enough.

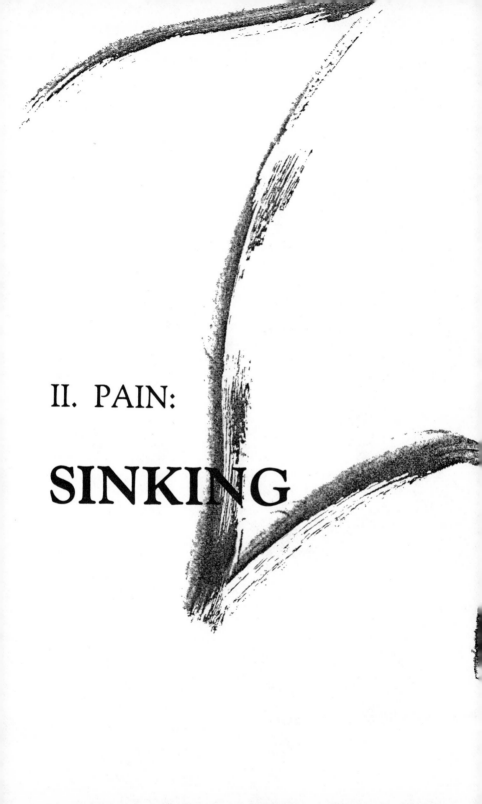

II. PAIN:

SINKING

Do you wish to have love?
    If
        you wish to have love,
   then
        you must leave
          love.

The soul does as pilgrims do who have eagerly climbed to
the summit of a mountain: they descend with care
lest they fall over a precipice.
    So it is with the soul:
On fire with its long love,
overpowered by the embrace of the Holy Trinity,
       it begins to sink
       and to cool—
As the sun from its highest zenith
       sinks down into the night,
       thus also, do we sink,
       soul and body.

There comes a time
    when both body and soul
       enter into such a vast darkness

that one loses light
    and consciousness
    and knows nothing more
       of God's intimacy.

At such a time
    when the light in the lantern burns out
      the beauty of the lantern
      can no longer be seen.

With longing and distress
    we are reminded
      of our nothingness.

At such a time I pray to God:
  "Lord, this burden is too heavy for me!"
And God replies:
  "I will take this burden first
      and clasp it close to Myself
      and that way
      you may more easily
      bear it."

But still I feel
    that I can bear no longer
    the wounds God has given me,
    unanointed and unbound.
My enemies surround me.
    O Lord, how long must I remain here on earth
    in this mortal body
    as a target at which people
        throw stones and shoot
    and assail my honor
        with their evil cunning?

I am hunted,
        captured,
                bound,
wounded so terribly
that I can never be healed.

God has wounded me
close unto death.
If God leaves me unanointed
I could never recover.
> Even if all the hills flowed with healing oils,
> and all the waters contained healing powers,
> and all the flowers
>> and all the trees
> dripped with healing ointments,
Still,
I could never recover.

Lord,
>   I will tear the heart of my soul in two
>   and you must lay therein.
>   You must lay yourself
>   in the wounds of my soul.

I am ill
    and I long deeply
        for the health-giving draught
        which Jesus Christ himself drank.

And he drank of it so deeply
    that he was on fire
        with love.

God replied:

    I wish always to be your physician,
    bringing healing anointment for all your
        wounds.

If it is I who allow you to be wounded so badly,
    do you not believe that I will heal you most
        lovingly
    in the very same hour?

From suffering I have learned this:
>That whoever
>>is sore wounded by love
>will never be made whole
>>unless
>>she embrace the very same love
>which wounded her.

Life without sorrow
    would be fool's folly.
        That is why
            God Himself
        took this path, one of sorrow and pain.
        God shows us that it is still
        a wonderful,

            noble,

                and holy way.

Only one without great guilt or sin
    suffers pain.

Love the nothing,
flee the self.
Stand alone.
Seek help from no one.
Let your being be quiet,
Be free from the bondage of all things.
Free those who are bound,
Give exhortation to the free.
Care for the sick
but dwell alone.
When you drink the waters of sorrow
you shall kindle the fire of love
with the match of perseverance —
    This is the way
        to dwell in the desert.

When my burdens and sufferings
    are held in front of me,
my soul begins to burn with a fire of true divine love
    and even my body soars in divine bliss.

And when I can no longer bear my loneliness
    I take it to my friends
    for I must share it with all the friends of God.

"Do you suffer?"
"So do I!"

Spiritual persons who dwell on earth
    are offered two kinds of spirit:
    In this way two pure natures come together,
        the first is
            the flowing Fire of the Godhead
    And the second is
            the gradual growth and expansion
            of the loving soul.

Our childhood was foolish
    our youth troubled

Alas!

    Now, in my old age I find much to criticize,
    for it can produce no shining works;
    it can be cold and without grace.
    Life appears powerless
    now that it no longer has youth
    to help it endure
        the fiery love of God.
    It is impatient —
    little ills afflict it much
    which in youth it noticed hardly at all.

Yes,

    a good old age must be full of patient waiting
    and trusts in God alone.

Remember this:
    That when our Lord
        releases the soul

   it sinks down
        and gives him thanks,
        even for this.

Thus it is
> that those who would storm the heavenly
>> heights
> by fierceness
> and ascetic practices
> deceive themselves badly.

Such people
> carry grim hearts within themselves,
> they lack true humility
> which alone
>> leads the soul to God.

In this fashion we learn the power
and the strength
of silence.

We learn to go into the world
as still as a mouse
in the depths of our heart.

When I open my heart
I find
Truth and Discretion
in all things.

God has so enfolded the soul
    into him/herself
    and so poured out the divine nature
        completely into it

that the soul is rendered speechless.
    It says nothing
    except that God is in the closest communion
        with it
    and God is more than a Father.

God says:
> Do not fear your death.
> For when that moment arrives
> I will draw my breath
>> and your soul will come to Me
>> like a needle
>>> to a magnet.

III. CREATIVITY:

AWAKENING

Woman!
 Your soul has slept from childhood on.
Now,
  it is awakened
   by the light of true love.
 In this light
   the soul looks around her
   To discover who it is
 Who is showing Himself to her here.
Now,
  she sees clearly
  she recognizes for the first time
  How
   God
    is All
     in All.

As soon as the soul
          begins to grow
     the dust of sin
        falls away
   and the soul becomes
             a god with God.
Then,
       what God wills
          the soul wills.
Otherwise,
     God and soul
        would not be united
        in so beautiful a union.

I once heard the Spirit speak to the Creator, saying:

"We will no longer be unfruitful!
We will have
a creative kingdom."

And then I heard Jesus speak to the Creator, saying:

"My nature too must bear fruit.
Together we shall work wonders
So let us fashion human beings
After the Pattern of myself."

Wherever genius
            combines wisdom
                    and love,
    There
            creation bears fruit.

The Holy Spirit flows
through us
with the marvelous
Creative Power
of everlasting joy!

As the Godhead
      strikes the note
   Humanity sings.
The Holy Spirit is the harpist
And all the strings must sound
   which are strung in love.

God lays the soul
            in his glowing heart
            so that He, the great God,
            and she, the humble maid,
embrace
and are united as thoroughly
as water is with wine.

As love grows and expands in the soul,
    it rises eagerly to God
        and overflows
            towards the Glory
   which bends towards it.

    Then Love melts through the soul
        into the senses,
   so that the body too might share in it,
for Love
    is drawn
        into all things.

Where love dwells,
there will I dwell.

The true blessing of God
    flows from the heavenly flood
        out of the spring of the flowing Trinity.

This flowing
    contains such power
        that it takes all strength from the body
        and lays the soul
        naked to itself.

Divine Love is so immensely great!
Great is its overflow,
for Divine Love is never still.
Always ceaselessly and tirelessly
  it pours itself out
  so that the small vessel which is ourselves
  might be filled to the brim
  and might also overflow.

The rippling tide of love
flows secretly
out from God
into the soul
And draws it mightily back
to its Source.

We are invited by God in the following manner:

"Fly, dove-winged one,
and soar in all things
beyond yourself.
And when you are tired and weary
Return to the flood again."

God speaks:

When your Easter comes
I shall be all around you,
I shall be through and through you
And I shall steal your body
And give you to your Love.

Humanity speaks:

> Lord!
> It would be wise
> to spare the body
> in which your Divine breath from the depths of the
> > Holy Trinity
> floated so sweetly down
> and pulsed so powerfully through the soul.

For

> if the body should lose its power
> men and women
> would become

> > > unfruitful.

Love
     wanders about
         through the senses
and then it
     storms the soul with all its powers.

In the heart of this maid
     I saw a spring of living water
     welling up.

Thus speaks a beggar woman
     in her prayer.

I am forced to write these words
     regarding which I would have gladly kept silent
     because I fear greatly the power of vainglory.
But,
     I have learned
          to fear more the judgment of God
     should I,
          God's little creature,
             keep silent.

I rise up with power.
    My glory is
        and will be manifold.

For everything that ever loves
    must praise this soul
    till it comes to the divine place
    of my Holy Trinity
    and there works such wonders
    that it flows
        and moves
            and charms
                and makes
                for love.

From the overflowing love of God
there flows evermore
into the soul
a sweet,
longing,
hungry,
love.

What is the greatest kind of love?

Great love

    does not flow with tears.

Rather,

    it burns in the great Fire of Heaven.

In this Fire
    it flows and flows swiftly
    yet all the while
    it remains in itself
    in a very great stillness.

God says:

     My glorious Divinity

  flows

    from hour

      to hour

  into

    your soul.

When I flow,

      you must race.

Thou shalt burn
    and never be extinguished
    like a living spark
        in the great Fire
            of the living Majesty.

If one blows
    even on the tiniest spark
        it gives forth both heat
            and light in the fire of heaven
        where all the radiant saints abide.

O lovely rose on the thorn,
      thou are sweet as the grape.
      A flower of great delight
      Yet the root of your constancy
      is in the Holy Spirit
      ever fresh and ever green.

Poor fool that I am,
> God pours me out the host's own wine
> which he himself has drunk.
> From this wine
> I become so overpowered
> that what the spirit then sings inwardly
> sounds sweeter by far
> than any earthly song.

It becomes
> a lyre to my ears,
> a voice for my words.

Come, dear friend,
I await you
and my heart
goes out to meet you.
I, though God,
lose myself
in you.

Who is God?

    God is

        the meaning for my joy.

    God is

        a gladsome joy to my being.

One day I saw
      with the eyes of my eternity
      in bliss and without effort,

                          a Stone.

This stone
      was like a great mountain
      and was of assorted colors.
      It tasted sweet, like heavenly herbs.
      I asked the sweet stone: Who are you?
It replied:
      I am Jesus.

God is not only fatherly.
God is also mother
    who lifts her loved child
    from the ground to her knee.

The Trinity is like a mother's cloak
wherein the child finds a home
and lays its head on the maternal breast.

God promises:

> You shall dance merrily
> manly in your strivings,
> yet remaining a maiden.

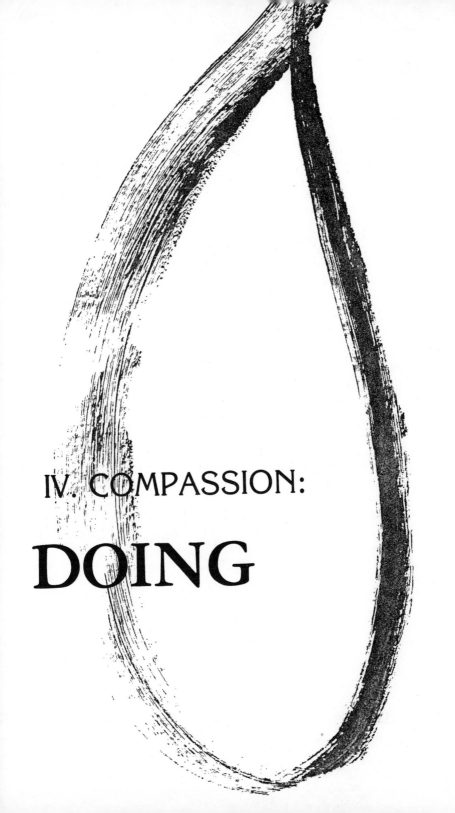

IV. COMPASSION:

DOING

God has given me

the power

to change my ways.

Do you wish to know my meaning?
Then lie down in the Fire.
See
    and taste
        the Flowing Godhead
        through your being.
Feel the Holy Spirit
    Moving
        and compelling
    you within the flowing
    Fire
        and Light
            of God.

God says:
> My love
>> bids you to work.

Whoever
> wishes to follow God in honest works
>> must never
>> stand still
> but must always
>> travel on.

Leap!
Leap in ordered dance —
Be a vanquisher
of evil spirits!

If you love the justice of Jesus Christ
    more than you fear human judgment
        then you will seek to do compassion.
Compassion means
    that if I see my friend and my enemy
    in equal need,
    I shall help both equally.
Justice demands
    that we seek
        and find the stranger,
    the broken, the prisoner
    and comfort them
        and offer them our help.

Here lies the holy compassion of God
    that causes the devils much distress.

Who is the Holy Spirit?
>The Holy Spirit is a compassionate outpouring
>>of the Creator
>>>and the Son.

This is why
>when we on earth
>>pour out compassion and mercy
>>from the depths of our hearts
>and give to the poor
>and dedicate our bodies to the service of the
>>broken,
>to that very extent
>do we resemble the Holy Spirit.

The noblest joy of the senses,
  the holiest peace of the heart,
      the most resplendent luster of all good
      works
  derives from this:
      that the creature
      puts his or her heart
      wholly into what s/he does.

When are we like God?

I will tell you.

> In so far as we love compassion
> and practice it steadfastly,
> to that extent
> do we resemble the heavenly Creator
> who practices these things
> ceaselessly in us.

For compassion
   comforts the sad,
      heals the wounded,
         and gladdens the hearts
    of all
    who come to her.
Each of us who seeks compassion
   and calls upon compassion resolutely
       conquers the sorrow and
       depression
    that lie in our heart.

Love transforms.
    Love makes empty hearts overflow.
    This happens even more
    when we have to struggle through
    without assurance,
    all unready
        for the play
           of Love.

Half of our good works
   and virtuous acts
is a gift from God.
Half
belongs to ourselves.

We can
        and we ought
                to make use
                of everything
                        that comes our way.

Stay by me.

   Support me.

      That I may diligently

serve the broken,
and bear the cost of such service

   in my goods
   and in my body.

Listen to this divine call:

> You shall loose those who are bound,
> You shall exhort the free,
> You shall care for the broken,
> You shall enlighten and teach,
> Yet in all this
> > you shall
> > > dwell alone.

How should one live?
Live
welcoming
to all.

What should you do?
  Do good by doing compassion
  to everyone
  you know needs it.
  Expect adversity.
  Bear adversity with love.

Do not shun power
    nor despise it.
    But use it correctly.
        When is power used correctly?
    Power is made for service.
    I am your servant;
        I am not your master.
Be a servant.
Not a master.

Heal the broken
    with comforting words of God.
    Cheer them gently
        with earthly joys.
Be merry
    and laugh with the broken
and carry their secret needs
in the deepest silence of your heart.

Do not judge others.
    Stand by them with love.
    Then God will lead them
    to be open to you
    and to themselves
    and to God.

When we get to heaven
    we shall find
    that there everything is held
    for the good of all in common.

Lord God,
    close now your treasured gift
    by a holy end.